W9-BMU-835

CONNECTING THE DOTS

W.W. NORTON & COMPANY

NEW YORK • LONDON

CONNECTING

THE

DOTS

P   O   E   M   S

MAXINE KUMIN

For information about permission to reproduce
selections from this book, write to Permissions,
W. W. Norton & Company, Inc., 500 Fifth Avenue,
New York, NY 10110.
The text of this book is composed in Garamond No. 3
with the display set in Garamond No. 3 Bold
Composition by Crane Typesetting Service, Inc.
Manufacturing by The Courier Companies, Inc.
Book design by JAM Design

Library of Congress Cataloging-in-Publication Data

Kumin, Maxine, date
      Connecting the dots : poems / Maxine Kumin.
        p.   cm.
      ISBN 0-393-03962-5
      I. Title.
   PS3521.U638C66   1996
   811'.54—dc20   95-44441

W. W. Norton & Company, Inc., 500 Fifth Avenue, New York, N.Y. 10110
http://web.wwnorton.com
W. W. Norton & Company Ltd., 10 Coptic Street, London WC1A 1PU

1   2   3   4   5   6   7   8   9   0

in loving memory of
Jane Kenyon
1947–1995

CONTENTS

ACKNOWLEDGMENTS

Grateful acknowledgment is made to the editors of the following periodicals, where some of the poems in this manuscript originally appeared, sometimes in slightly different form: *The Atlanta Review, The Atlantic, Columbia, The Formalist, Green Mountains Review, The Hudson Review, Mirabella, Ms., The Nation, The Paterson Literary Review, Ploughshares, Poetry* (Chicago), *Prairie Schooner, Tikkun, Tri-Quarterly, Wilderness, Witness.*

The title poem, "Connecting the Dots," was first published in *Switched-On Gutenberg,* an electronic poetry journal on the Internet.

"The Bridge-Builder" has appeared in the *Routledge Anthology of Cross-Gendered Verse* (Routledge) 1996.

"Getting the Message" was commissioned by Auburn Theological Seminary for their 175th anniversary event. It also appears in *The Best American Poetry 1995* (Scribners).

"Gus Speaks" first appeared in *Unleashed: Poems by Writers' Dogs* (Crown) 1995.

"The Word" was reprinted in *Women, Animals, and Vegetables* (Norton) 1994.

"New Year's Eve 1959" first appeared in the anthology *Literary Olympians,* 1992.

I

·

·

·

LETTERS

"Dear Muzz," I wrote, the summer I was ten
from a seedy nature camp in the Poconos
with cows and calves, huge geese, some half-wild ponies
—heaven for the urban savage I was then—
"I have to do this letter to get breakfast.
Kiss Kerry for me. I milked a cow named Clover."
(Kerry, my dog, already dead, run over
the week I left.) Muzz from the bosomy British
matron in charge of spunky orphans who reclaim
the family's fortunes in a book I adored.
My older brothers called you Dolly, cleared
as almost-adults to use your cute nickname.
"Dear Muzz, with love" however smudged and brief
from your animal, sole daughter in your life.

Your animal, sole daughter in your life,
I mourned my dog, the slaughter of Clover's calf.
You were born Bella, number six of twelve.
The butter was spread too thin, childhood too brief
shared with Eva, Sara, Lena, Esther, Saul,
Meyer, Nathan, Oscar, Dan, Jay, Joe.
The younger ones mewed to be held by you.
The older ones, above your crib, said "doll."
You made me your confessor. At eighteen
you eloped, two virgins fleeing Baltimore,
buttoned in one berth by a Pullman porter
who jollied your tears at breakfast next morning
before the train pulled into Buffalo.
Your face announced Just Married, you blushed so.

Just married, one day pregnant, you blushed so
pink Niagara's fabled sunset paled.
"Papá will kill me when he hears," you quailed
but the first grandchild, a boy, softened the blow.
You told me how your mother had slapped your face
the day your first blood caked along your thighs,
then sent you to your sister for advice.
Luckier, I was given *Marjorie May's*
Twelfth Birthday, a vague tract printed by Kotex,
so vague it led me to believe you bled
that one year only, and chastely left unsaid
the simple diagrammatics about sex.
When was it that I buried Muzz, began
to call you by the name that blazoned Woman?

I came to call you Dolly, The Other Woman,
the one I couldn't be. I was cross-eyed,
clumsy, solitary, breasts undersized.
Made wrong. An orthodontist's dream. A bookworm.
That winter, a houseguest, his wife gone shopping,
pinned me in my bedroom by the mirror
and as we both watched, took out to my horror
a great stiff turkey neck, a hairless thing
he wanted to give me. How could I tell you this,
how he pressed against me, put it in my hand,
groped my nipples, said, "Someday you'll understand"?
How tell you, who couldn't say vagina, penis?
This isn't recovered memory. I never forgot it.
I came to call you Dolly. That's when it started.

At 14, I called you Dolly. The war had started,
absorbing my brothers one by one. The first-
born fought in Rommel's Africa, then crossed
to the Italian Boot. Your cocktail parties
grew shriller that year, the air more fiercely mortal
as the second son went off to ferry bombers
over the Burma Hump. Your hair, by summer,
began to thin, then fell out, purgatorial.
The youngest, apple of your eye, was shot
down in the Pacific, plucked from his atoll
and survived with a pair of shattered ankles.
You had to wear a wig. I dared to gloat.
The rage of adolescence bit me deep.
I loathed your laugh, your scarves, your costly makeup.

Your laugh, your scarves, the gloss of your makeup,
shallow and vain. I wore your lips, your hair,
even the lift of my eyebrows was yours
but nothing of you could please me, bitten so deep
by the fox of scorn. Like you, I married young
but chose animals, wood heat, hard hours
instead of Sheffield silver, freshcut flowers,
your life of privilege and porcelain.
My children came, the rigorous bond of blood.
Little by little our lives pulled up, pulled even.
A sprinkle here and there of approbation:
we both agreed that what I'd birthed was good.
How did I come to soften? How did you?
Goggy is what my little ones called you.

Goggy, they called you, basking in the sun
of your attention. You admired their ballet;
their French; their algebra; their Bach and Debussy.
The day the White House rang you answered, stunned
your poet-daughter was wanted on the phone
—the Carters' party for a hundred bards.
We shopped together for the dress I'd wear.
Our rancors melted as ocean eases stone.
That last year of your life, the names you thought of:
Rogue, Doc, Tudor, Daisy, Garth,
the horses of your lost Virginia youth.
You said them, standing in my barn, for love.
Dying, you scratched this fragment for me, a prize;
"Darling . . . your visit . . . even . . . so brief . . . Muzz."

THE HEIGHT OF THE SEASON

Once a time is how the baby asks for a story
wandering from person to person patiently seeking
a teller of Three Bears or Riding Hood to take him in.
Clutching the book he pleads with his nine-year-old cousin
Once a time? Have it? meaning to solve the mystery
of words he has come to love but cannot unlock.

Once when my father's heart was starting to stop
I took him blackberry jam and we sat in his cubicle
in the Pennsylvania Graduate Hospital
spreading its sugar on saltines, not so much
a study in contrasts as a way safely to touch.
I was glad that my father had died, his optimism
intact, the year before Jack Kennedy was shot
and Jackie sat wiping his blood and brains from her suit.
Glad that my father was spared that televised vision.

In once a time a different language is spoken.
The landscape is sweet there, free of briar or bracken.
The animals talk in reasonable tones that children
can understand. As tonight at the stove three women
converse over berries, mashing the afternoon's pickings
with sugar in the pot. This is the height of the season,
ripeness enfolds us. My daughters and I remember
the absent enthusiast, the goddess, my mother
who sieved seeds from gallons of pulp with a fervor
we cannot match, though we long to extend the continuum.

Meanwhile at the kitchen table a game begins
with dice and six counters and a book of questions.
The categories are constant: always Sports,
Geography, Current Events, History and the Arts
(largely cinema stars the vintage of Liz Taylor),

a game the nine-year-old is intent on winning
while the baby wanders from player to player inquiring
have it? and wax is melted to seal the jars.
A benevolent rain swells tomorrow's cucumbers
and reddening tomatoes (what else must I save?)
as the axis turns, spilling us into fall
until, in tears now with his have it?
the tired baby will have it all.

AFTER THE CLEANSING OF BOSNIA

Tonight again they walk up to
the hills, they walk on canes
or crutches or in ancient overshoes
to wait for food to fall from planes
and fight for it, be stabbed or shot.

Still, dozing in the cottony light
of 5 a.m., I can pretend to snatch you
out of the chosen life you wake to.
Sometimes I rewrite where you are,
expatriate daughter. I can almost cancel
the haunted days last fall
you rode in an armored personnel carrier
turtling into the destroyed towns
leveled the way God damned
Sodom and Gomorrah. In Vukovar,
you said, a city of 30,000,
only two roofs stood. You ran your hand
over miles of houses pebbled down to sand

but what I shut my eyes on were
Cape Cod's childhood flats
where, sneakered against razor clam cuts,
we daily dowsed for treasure
and bore it home in buckets.

I spy you ten years back
flooded with refugees in Bangkok.
You toured the notorious
camps, counseled the hopeless,
dickered and cajoled
to win spaces
for the unplaceable
from the Danes, the Dutch,
the Belgians, the generous

Canadians. You rocked
the naked girl child thought
to be three years old,
sole survivor of pirates
who swept the seas
clean of hated Vietnamese.

Years before that, in Haiti,
your first poor shattered country,
you scoured the upland bush by *vélo*
conducting a census for UNESCO.
The *blanc* you were—
a word for foreigner,
any color, any gender—
lay down to sleep in huts,
was stoical on straw mats
scratching and sweating
under mosquito nets.
You scrounged bananas along the way,
changed your tampon behind a tree
and fueled the engine of
your moral outrage. Love
helped it sputter and catch.
I see the gears still mesh.

> *Don't read that page, it's too poor, you said*
> *covering the picture of the merrygoround pony*
> *who ran away from the carousel and got lost*
> *in the dark and then you thumbed ahead*
> *to where the story ended.*

How tender the earth is under all this snow
on our side, 97 inches since November
and over there since November in heavy snow
the food stocks dwindling until surely
the whole world must notice how slowly
the dying progresses. When the convoy
is turned back, when children
are trampled to death in the bed of the truck,

hundreds pressed upright flank to flank
crueler than cattle carted to market,
when even the hostile soldiers take
pity and throw up snow to suck,
when even the hostile soldiers throw back
bewildered babies that have dropped
from the arms of exhausted women, how tender
the earth is and we on it face up.

Last night I dreamed we both looked up
into the arms of a vast snowy hemlock
in time to see our old barn owl alight,
a mouse in his talons. He sat
nodding his heartshaped face at us,
tore the head apart, devoured this
and launched himself soundlessly.
We saw the great brooding wings hump by.
We felt the empty air rush back.
We saw there was no obstacle
he-who-looks-behind-without-looking,
he-who-looks-ahead-without-blinking
could not thread through, backward or forward,
and we were falsely comforted.

GETTING THE MESSAGE

God, the rabbis tell us, never assigns
exalted office to a man until
He has tested his mettle in small things.
So it is written in the Midrash
that when a lamb escaped the flock Moses
overtook it at a brook drinking its fill
and said, I would have taken thee in my arms
and carried thee thither had I known thy thirst
whereupon a Heavenly Voice warmly
resounded, *As thou livest, thou art fit.*

Divine election's scary. The burning bush
might have been brightened by St. Elmo's fire
according to *The Interpreter's One-Volume
Commentary.* The slopes of Exodus,
scrub growth close-cropped by tough horned herds
of Jacob's sheep (now prized as an heirloom breed)
lack treetops, mountain peaks or spires
that might discharge electrical ghost-plumes.
St. Elmo's seems less science than the desire
of modern exegetes to damp the flame.

I like my Bible tales, like Scotch, straight up,
incontrovertible as Dante's trip
through seven circles, Milton's map
of Paradise or Homer's wine-dark epic.
On such a stage there falls a scrim between
text and critique where bursts of light may crack
and dance as if on masts of sailing ships
and heavenly voices leap from alp to plain.
In Sunday School I shivered at God's command:
Take off thy shoes, thou stand'st on holy ground

and lay awake in the hot clutch of faith
yearning yet fearful that the Lord might speak

to me in my bed or naked in my bath.
I didn't know how little risk I ran
of being asked to set my people free
from fording some metaphorical Red Sea
with a new-sprung Pharaoh raging at my back.
I didn't know the patriarchy that spared me
fame had named me chattel, handmaiden.
God's Angels looked me over but flew by.

I like to think God's talent scouts today
select for covenant without regard
for gender, reinterpreting The Word
so that holy detectives glossing the bush
(most likely wild acacia), scholars of J
E and P deciphering Exodus
will fruitfully research the several ways
divine authentication lights up truth.
Fragments of it, cryptic, fugitive
still spark the synapses that let us live.

REHEARSING FOR THE FINAL
RECKONING IN BOSTON

During the Berlioz *Requiem* in Symphony Hall
which takes even longer than extra innings
in big league baseball, this restless Jewish agnostic
waits to be pounced on, jarred by the massed fanfare
of trombones and trumpets assembling now in the second
balcony, left side, right side, and at the rear.

Behind them, pagan gods in their niches
acoustically oversee this most Christian
of orchestrations: the resting Satyr
of Praxiteles, faun with infant Bacchus,
Apollo Belvedere, Athena, Diana
of Versailles with early greyhound.

When the wild mélange cries out
Dies irae, all of our bared hearts pulse
under Ozawa's baton. He is lithe as a cat,
nimble as Nureyev, another expatriate.
But even Ozawa dressed in white sweats
cannot save us up here in peanut heaven, or save

patrons downstairs in the best seats canted back
for the view, who wear the rapt faces of the fifties
tilted to absorb the movie on the 3-D screen.
Naught shall remain unavenged, sings the chorus.
*What trembling there shall be when we rise again
to answer at the throne.* That's all of us

since Adam, standing on one another's shoulders
three or four deep, I should imagine,
acrobats of the final reckoning.
And what terror awaits those among us
whose moral priorities are unattached
to Yahweh, Allah, Buddha, Christ:

forgiving without praying for forgiveness,
the doing unto others, scrubbing toilets,
curbing lust, not taking luck for granted?
Are the doubters reckoned up or just passed over?
Hector was almost passed over, his *Requiem*
unplayed, save for a general killed in battle . . .

How should one dress for the Day of Judgment?
At a working rehearsal the chorus is motley,
a newborn *fin de siècle* in t-shirts and jeans.
But what will they wear when the statues have crumbled
in 2094? Brasses and massive tympani close
the *Lacrymosa*. Metallic spittle is hot in my throat.

Now we enter the key of G major, the Lamb
of God key of catharsis and resolution.
Like a Janus head looking backward and forward,
pockmarked by doubt I slip between cymbals
to the other side of the century where our children's
children's children ride out on the ranting brasses.

YOUTH ORCHESTRA, WITH DOGS

University of the South

On the day that Sarajevo falls
a gang of music-loving mongrels
scraggy, loosely arranged
and mysteriously ownerless
lolls panting by the junior harpist
who plucks bright sprigs of Vivaldi
under one of the Gothic arches
that knit these slabs of pale sandstone
into a medieval surround.

Cellists, oboists, French horn
players settle themselves at random
among the Civil War oaks.
Against the resolute
machinery of three thousand cicadas
and the deep flank-snufflings
of a dozen grinning mutts
barefoot teens on a dappled lawn
rehearse, drop pages, start again.

Mahler is ragged. A smoother Mozart.
Arpeggios drift past all afternoon.
Such concentration is required
to stay in time. . . . Years ago
I ferried drums, cellos, children
to rehearsals, saved seven dogs
the pound prepared to gas, took in
a foster son thrust up by an earlier war. . . .
What was it the freelance photographer

said in her helmet and flak vest? *We*
zoomed in on exploded arms and legs,
instant orphans, blownup pets
and god! who cares? In the aftermath
humanitarians airlift damaged babies

to surgeries and skin grafts
in safe countries. Once they're healed
the doctors pledge to send them back.
Now it is evening. The old city is black.

Here on the Episcopalian plain
that once shunned women, Jews, and colored skin,
an orchestra containing all assembles.
The first violinist, sincerely
sixteen in a Laura Ashley print,
arrives on stage to modest applause.
The Adam's-apple conductor raises
his baton. Members in vigorous unison
embark on Copland's "Appalachian Spring."

CROSS-COUNTRY SKIING

I love to be lured under the outstretched wings
of hemlocks heavily snowed upon, the promise
of haven they hold seductively out of the wind
beckoning me to stoop under, tilt my face
to the brashest bits that sift through. Sequestered,
I think how in the grainy videos
of refugees, snow thick as flaking plaster
falls on their razed villages. Snow
forms a cunning scrim through which the ill-clad
bent under bundles of bedding and children appear
nicely muted, trudging slow motion to provide
a generic version of misery and terror
for those who may step out of their skis to sit
under hemlock wings in all-American quiet.

II

-
-
-

THE BRIDGE-BUILDER

June 17, 1848. *Charles Ellet, Jr., the civil engineer who designed the
suspension bridge soon to be built over Niagara Falls, today tested the
service span to be used in its construction by driving his horse across the
planking.* Brooklyn Eagle

I, Charles Ellet, Jr., licensed engineer
son of a provident Quaker farmer
now stand at the gorge where Niagara Falls

offers a prospect so sublime no rival
as yet is known on this great globe of ours.
Let men deride me as actor, rain-maker;

let it be said of me that I have loved
all carriageways and catwalks, all defiles
wide gaps and narrow verges to be bridged

am fond of women and horses equally
although the latter's sensibility
is plainer far to read. However much

respect I hold for Nature's rash downrush
her virginal ebullience, I itch
to take it in the compass of my fingers.

One does not "break" a horse, but wins its trust.
With towers and cables, not brute trusses;
with tact, not tug; suspension, not piled piers

I mean to overarch this wild splendor.

•   •   •

Let them think me odd who see as if
asleep my silent self reflecting how
to span the rapids boiling at my feet

two hundred forty feet below the cliff
to be exact. An arrow from a bow?
A bird or a balloon? Why not a kite?

A kite could soar across the open rift!
The public loves such deeds. I'll offer a prize
a decent sort of prize, say five gold dollars

to the first man or boy who sends his string
to Canada. The placard up three days
a local gaptoothed lad steps forth to win—

a widow's son, shy skinny Homan Walsh.
He's going to outlive me. Will he grow
up bold, race Thoroughbreds, get rich

performing acts of wild derring-do?
I never will find out, but know that I'm
to die a colonel in the Civil War

a hero slain leading a charge of rams
—warships rigged to ram opponents' hulls—
on The Big Muddy to rout the Confederates.

•   •   •

Backward looks are licensed. To look for-
ward isn't done; is not acceptable.
But give me leave to leap beyond the date

of my flamboyance, 1848
and introduce High-Jumping Sam: Sam Patch
clad all in white, who dives from the cliff into

the rainbowed pool at the foot of the cataract
and not content with one dive, makes it two.
Reprises at Genesee and straightway drowns.

Or Blondin in '59 adored by thousands
who cheer his tightrope walk across the chasm.
He'll have a score of successors, circus clowns

who mock the danger, simulate cold fear
half-fall, recover and go blithely on
some piggyback, some skipping rope, afire

with the same lust for fame and fortune
as those who dare chute down the drop in barrels.
The first a cooper proving his staves would hold

then scores of imitators taking the falls
by barrel, boat and cork, a steady parade
Of madmen. And always the suicides . . .

Dramatic death! Love also knows no season.
Though bliss be brief that attends unbridled passion
romantic couples will hasten by canal

or rail to flaunt their ecstatic portion
fulfill the fleeting period of joy
that one wag titles "honey-lunacy."

Some say the Falls gently distract the lovers'
overweening focus on one another.
Some say the tumult of the cataract

conceals the newlyweds' embarrassment
caught, as it were, in the rapturous nuptial act.
Others aver the Falls' ceaseless descent

evokes a rich manly response. Some brides
claim happy negative ions are produced
by falling water. You may take your choice

of savants, sages and hypotheses
but thus Niagara will come to boast
hotels and curio shops and carriage-rides

to vistas for photos of the just-now wived.
Skeptic I am, unmarried by design.
Still, might not the spectacle conjoin

male and female qualities into one?

•   •   •

Now let us turn back from this clairvoyant
glimpse to the day that Homan's kitestring held.
I tie it to a somewhat stouter cord

and next, a heavier one of finespun wire
and ever mightier cables to support
stout wooden planks until from shore to shore

just wide enough to let a phaeton pass
a catwalk spans the gorge. The boards are spaced
to let rainwater through. Side rails? None.

I test it harshly across and back, first at
a walk, then jog, then crow-hop up and down
assured that it will hold. Once *I* trust it

I harness up my mare, to show *she* will.
A chestnut Morgan, foaled in my own barn
and trained to voice commands the way a skilled

driving horse need be, to keep from harm.
Vixen by name but not by temperament
spirited, willing and confident.

Do not mistake submission, the highest
accolade man can bestow on a horse
with truckling subservience. The mare must trust

the steady justice of the driver's hand.
Fingers that speak, not snatch; a voice
that soothes and urges but withholds choice.

Vixen and I prepare to take our stand.
I, upright in the cart as in a chariot
the better she may sense we are allied

ask her to move off at a rapid trot.
She never casts a glance to either side.
The crowd is aghast. Several women swoon.

The catwalk sways most fearfully but holds
beneath the mare and horseman in the sky
and that is how we cross, Vixen, my bold

partner and I, Charles Ellet, Jr.
bridge-builder, licensed engineer.

THE LAST WORDS OF HENRY MANLEY

At first I thought I heard wrong. Was she sayen
Oil History Project, maybe somethen
about the year I put in ditchen, layen
roadbed up Stark Mountain in the CCC?
Liven alone, I'm shy of company
but then this girl comes prettied up in blue jeans
and has me talk into a tape machine
about my raisen. Seems it's history.

I was the raisen boy of Old Man Wasson.
Back then, the county farmed out all its orphans
to any who would have them for their keep.
My ma and pa both died in World War One.
It was the influenza took them, took down
half the town. I cried myself to sleep
one whole year, I missed my ma so terrible.
I weren't but six and scrawny. Weren't able
to do much more than clean the chicken coop

and toss hay to the goats. I weren't much good
but Old Man Wasson never used me wrong.
Because he lived alone, there were some said
he weren't right upstairs, and then they'd nod.
He fed me up on eggs and goat's milk, taught
me thirty different birds to know by song
and every plant that came. First one's coltsfoot.
Lambs' quarters is good to eat. So's cattail shoots.
Cobwebs is for cuts. Jewelweed's for the sting
of nettles. Asters bloom last. Most everythen

we ate we grew. And bartered for the rest
hayen in summer, all fall choppen wood.
Whilst I was small I stacked as best I could:
hickory, oak, maple, ash. (White birch
is only fit for tourists from the city.)

I saved my dimes for the county fair. Went dressed
up clean in Sunday clothes as if for church,
a place we never went nor never prayed.
We was a scandal to the Ladies Aid.

If there's one thing I still can't stand it's pity.
We had a handpump in the yard, a privy
a cookstove in the kitchen, a potbelly
in the front room, lamps enough to read by.
Kerosene burns yellow. I miss it still.
Not steady like a bulb, it's flickery
like somethen alive: a bird, a swallowtail.
You won't think that about 'lectricity.
And we had flowers too, old-timey ones

you hardly see these days, like hollyhocks
and red tobacco plants the hummenbirds
come to. Old Man Wasson had me listen
how those ruby throats would speak—chrk chrk—
to every bloom before they'd poke their beaks
inside. There's lots to say that don't need words.
I guess I was *his* father at the end.
He wouldn't have a doctor on the place.
I got in bed and held him till he went.

Winter of '44, private first class
in uniform like in the CCC
homesick and seasick I shipped across.
What made me famous was goen to the camps
where they'd outright starved most the men to death
and gassed the rest. Those piles of shoes and teeth?
They still come up. I dream them up in clumps.
Back home, the papers got aholt of me.
Local boy a hero in Germany.

Right here the tape clicks off. She says she's *thrilled.*
I want to say I've hardly started in
but she's packed up and standen on the doorsill
and I'm the boy whose time ran out for courten.

No one to hear me tell my other stories.
I never married. Wished I had. No roost
for this old turkey cock to share when the sun
goes down. I swung for the brass ring once, but missed
my chance. It happens. That's history.

III

.

.

.

IN A DIFFERENT COUNTRY

Music Festival, Sewanee, Tennessee

In come the harps, four grounded wings
as of some Cretaceous dragonfly
dismembered and shellacked:
two black, one cedar-red, one golden brown
conveyed on baggage dollies,
torn angels positioned one by one
al fresco in the sun

to be plucked by four dewy girls
ordered the way Matisse
might have arrayed them: a blonde
at the black, a black at the cedar-red
an Asian at the golden brown and
a pale brunette at the other black.
While we sit pampered in the shade

out pours the piece I came to grief on:
Karl Phillip Emanuel's "Solfeggietto."
Miss Alexander's spatulate digits
stretched my stubby fingers to enforce
leaps I couldn't make, little runs
through lesser unplayable Bach
that defeated me the year I was ten.

Parents, nostalgists, drop-ins hush.
The harps sing, it is virginal.
Karl Phillip two hundred years gone
and Miss Alexander misplaced fifty years
outside whose window even then
as now a cardinal from the pin
oak calls *fierce fierce*!

AN INSIDER'S VIEW OF THE GARDEN

How can I help but admire the ever perseverant
unquenchable dill
that sways like an unruly crowd at a soccer match
waving its lacy banners
where garlic belongs or slyly invading a hill
of Delicata squash—
how can I help but admire such ardor? I seek it

as bees the flower's core, hummingbirds
the concocted sugar water
that lures them to the feeder in the lilacs.
I praise the springy mane
of untamed tendrils asprawl on chicken wire
that promise to bring forth
peas to overflow a pillowcase.

Some days I adore my coltish broccolis,
the sketchbook beginnings
of their green heads still encauled, incipient trees
sprung from the Pleistocene.
Some days the leeks, that Buckingham Palace patrol
and the quarter-mile of beans
—green, yellow, soy, lima, bush and pole—

demand applause. As do dilatory parsnips,
a ferny dell of tops
regal as celery. Let me laud onion that erupts
slim as a grass stem
then spends the summer inventing its pungent tulip
and the army of brussels sprouts
extending its spoon-shaped leaves over dozens of armpits

that conceal what are now merely thoughts, mere nubbins
needing long ripening.
But let me lament my root-maggot-raddled radishes

my bony and bored red peppers
that drop their lower leaves like dancehall strippers
my cauliflowers that spit
out thimblesize heads in the heat and take beetles to bed.

O children, citizens, my wayward jungly dears
you are all to be celebrated
plucked, transplanted, tilled under, resurrected here
—even the lowly despised
purslane, chickweed, burdock, poke, wild poppies.
For all of you, whether eaten or extirpated
I plan to spend the rest of my life on my knees.

EARLY THOUGHTS OF WINTER

It's sweaty work, the getting ready part.
This winter's cordwood split and stacked
seen endwise is as gratifying
as the Pyramids in a steel engraving
each stone etched with equal emphasis.

Spraddle-legged in the humbling steam
of the manure pile I stand shoveling
pickup loads to tuck the garden in
dreaming beyond backache and tedium
of February with each dip, lift and fling

remembering Heidegger, his broad-jawed noun
Geworfenheit, for the castaway's condition
the shipwrecked seeker after news across
the water, the burrower, gleaner I need to be.

I summon up my winter Crusoe-self
the she-who-enters-her-own-stubbornness
who, chilled to rising in the predawn pitch
to stoke the stoves, will overhear the tick
and thrust of seeds inside the sleet's sad tune

and with the wild turkeys, the bachelor moose
the endearing cluster of juncos braving
the barn floor, comrade castaways
demand from February good news
across the water.

ALMOST SPRING, DRIVING HOME, RECITING HOPKINS

"A devout but highly imaginative Jesuit,"
Untermeyer says in my yellowed
college omnibus of modern poets,
perhaps intending an oxymoron, but is it?
Shook foil, sharp rivers start to flow.
Landscape plotted and pieced, gray-blue, snow-pocked
begins to show its margins. Speeding back
down the interstate into my own hills
I see them *fickle, freckled*, mounded fully
and softened by millennia into pillows.
The priest's sprung metronome tick-tocks,
repeating how old winter is. It asks
each mile, snow fog battening the valleys,
what is all this juice and all this joy?

AFTER THE HEAT WAVE

Rain falls down on the newly shorn sheep.
Deerflies lie doggo, black flies are absent.
Not one emerges from the great storehouse.
The barn cats are sleeping, birds are force-feeding
three clutches of phoebes, two of robins
and I am shelling the first of the season's
peas as a merciful summer rain
falls down all morning around me in strings.

CHORES

All day he's shoveled green pine sawdust
out of the trailer truck into the chute.
From time to time he's clambered down to even
the pile. Now his hair is frosted with sawdust.
Little rivers of sawdust pour out of his boots.

I hope in the afterlife there's none of this stuff
he says, stripping nude in the late September sun
while I broom off his jeans, his sweater flocked
with granules, his immersed-in-sawdust socks.
I hope there's no bedding, no stalls, no barn

no more repairs to the paddock gate the horses
burst through when snow avalanches off the roof.
Although the old broodmare, our first foal, is his,
horses, he's fond of saying, make divorces.
Fifty years married, he's safely facetious.

No garden pump that's airbound, no window a grouse
flies into and shatters, no ancient tractor's
intractable problem with carburetor
ignition or piston, no mowers and no chain saws
that refuse to start, or start, misfire and quit.

But after a Bloody Mary on the terrace
already frost-heaved despite our heroic efforts
to level the bricks a few years back, he says
let's walk up to the field and catch the sunset
and off we go, a couple of aging fools.

I hope, he says, on the other side there's a lot
less work, but just in case I'm bringing tools.

IN PRAISE OF THE NEW
TRANSFER STATION

How I love to go to the dump that is not the dump
I remember from the pre-ecological days
when we backed our pickup trucks as close to the edge
as we dared and hurled the detritus of our lives
into the smoldering pit rats flittered around.
Fire popped longnecked bottles that once held wine

and flags of escaping trash madly danced in the wind.
I remember the gray malaise attached to that dump
stirring something more than ashes and unburnt rind.
The town's teenage toughs hung out there in a daze
smoking pot, swapping girls, trying to jump-start their lives,
a motley assortment of mohawked Harrys and Eds

who ended up in the mill, each one at the edge
of a stack of hemlock the serrated sawblades whined
through, ripping the proximate boards as lightly as leaves.
It's a social occasion now to go to the dump
that is not a dump anymore, where on Saturdays
neighbors collect on the landscaped sward that surrounds

the recycle bins for aluminum, tin, the ground-
glass machine that sets everyone's teeth on edge
as it gobbles used jars to build roads with another day,
and neat pyramids of newsprint that will soon wind
up pulped for more news. Items we used to dump
are arrayed in the Recycle Hut like so many loaves

and fishes: Monopoly, bicycles seeking new lives,
toy trains and Barbies, barrows to wheel around,
while outside on a knoll at the dump that is not a dump
anymore, a sculpture of tires serves as a hedge
and under a clump of birches, scoured bright by the wind,
squat porcelain toilets and tubs that have seen better days.

You could cater a picnic here almost any day,
admire the sparkling used metal, how sunlight laves
and redeems clustered sundries that wait in the wind
to be weighed and carted away toward another round
of orderly reincarnation. Crocuses edge
the fenceline of the dump that's no longer a dump

and in a few days new sedge will spring up around
the castled stump pile where a dumpling chipmunk lives.
The lilacs of May will lightly perfume the wind.

THE WORD

We ride up softly to the hidden
oval in the woods, a plateau rimmed
with wavy stands of gray birch and white pine,
my horse thinking his thoughts, happy
in the October dapple, and I thinking
mine-and-his, which is my prerogative,

both of us just in time to see a big doe
loft up over the four-foot fence, her white scut
catching the sun and then releasing it,
soundlessly clapping our reveries shut.
The pine grove shivers as she passes.
The red squirrels thrill, announcing her departure.

Come back! I want to call to her,
we who mean you no harm. Come back and show us
who stand pinned in stopped time to the track
how you can go from a standing start
up and over. We on our side, pulses racing
are synchronized with your racing heart.

I want to tell her, Watch me
mornings when I fill the cylinders
with sunflower seeds, see how the chickadees
and lesser redbreasted nuthatches crowd
onto my arm, permitting me briefly
to stand in for a tree,

and how the vixen in the bottom meadow
I ride across allows me under cover
of horse scent to observe the education
of her kits, how they dive for the burrow
on command, how they re-emerge at another
word she uses, a word I am searching for.

Its sound is o-shaped and unencumbered,
the see-through color of river,
airy as the topmost evergreen fingers
and soft as pine duff underfoot
where the doe lies down out of sight;
take me in, tell me the word.

VIGNETTE

Every morning the Head Start van
rattles down the ruts of Poorhouse Road
to collect Emmet, who is first on
and last off and suffers from attention
deficit disorder but loves the schoolyard
slides and swings, lunchtime, and Sue, his driver.

Every afternoon where Poorhouse Road
spirals down to dirt, old foundered Radar
uproots himself from the muck of his pasture
and focusses his one good eye uphill.
The van pulls over. Emmet, clutching the apple
Sue unfailingly provides,
scrambles over the sagging fence rail.
No attention deficit on either side.

DÉJÀ VU

They met in a blackberry patch
before catapults, cannons or Spam.
Before longbows, the War of the Roses
and oh! it is true he was handsome.
He licked the blood from her scratches.
All too soon she went off with him
(the story is always the same)
to the kingdom of bitter surprises.

No thought of her parents, those furies,
once darkened their hedonic fancy.
No gendarmes, no CIA snooping.
The mosses they lay on were spongy.
All summer they dallied in briars,
fished brooks that gladdened them leaping.
He fed her on nine kinds of berries.
He fed her on salmon and honey.

By late fall when she married her bear
none could dispute her condition.
The winter cave they prepared
with its pallet of springy pine boughs
was cozy and amply proportioned.
They exchanged more tickles and vows
until he sank in a torpor
from which he could not be roused.

Denned up in that twilit world
she grew hairier, took to all fours.
When the baby was born (a girl)
she came to her senses. Of course
she still loved him! She loved the child!
But his smell was frankly distracting.
His grunts were driving her wild.
He said that the way she was acting

was bad for the cub. Soapy water
could not scour the birthmark of Ursus
from the breast of her darling daughter.
There were tears. Growls followed curses.
She left when the moon was a platter
of silver lighting the rises
and hollows that led, days later,
through thickets of furze and gorse

with the babe in her arms, to the castle
—six rooms, one full bath, one lav—
she had fled without suitcase or parcel,
a song on her lips, to her love.
Alas, it's the prick of the spindle
all over again. When this child
has grown to a toothsome bundle
with a heart that is ripe and wild,

in some woodland glade unseen
there are bound to be blackberries growing
beyond the strict reach of the queen
and a bear-prince will lurk there, all-knowing.
What will be already has been.

DOWN EAST NEWS ITEM

In a stove-in fifties Cadillac
crashed in a quarry west of Brunswick
two bear cubs and their matriarch
have taken up abode. The sow
dozes behind the wheel, the cubs
bask against the windshield. How
they got down there, most likely crab-
wise, scuttling when they dared
from shelf to shelf, we'll never know.

Since feckless humans hurl their garbage
down the rock face to be spared
composting it (though you might say
it gets composted either way
in time) the bears don't need to forage.
Here comes the satisfying splat
of rotted squash, the ratatat
of chicken bones, the tick of pans
still stickered with takeout dividends,
manna that raises a tatted crust
on fenders roseate with rust.

A dazzle of August sunlight sleeks
the tail fins into almost-motion
but later, when cold darkness licks
rime-deep into their twisted bastion
the sow will claw a ragged cave
in the upholstery stuffing
and maybe they'll all three survive
into another kingdom come.
Elsewhere General Motors hums.

ALLEGORIES IN H, D, AND B

H

If peace demands a lie
the Talmud says a lie's
permissible.
HONESTY
an old dog, pilfers
whatever morsels befall
then farts under the table.
We strike matches, fan the air
to dispel his rich retort
but truth is ever able
to outsmell even sulphur.

From time to time
she will appear as
the moment's prima ballerina
but like the lioness
trailed by her hyena
to the kill, her grand jetés
all too soon run down.
HAPPINESS
is everyone's chimera.

Neither beautiful nor lucky
HUMILITY
a brown bird
one of the lesser sparrows
rarely sings.
She is shy and swift of wing
camouflage her own reward
survival in her marrow.

HYPOCRISY
that clove-scented dentist
peers into her mouth
clucks his compassion but
readies the drill.
Blissed out on novocain
she hardly notices
the hollow that he's cut.
Then comes blood, comes pain
followed by the bill.

•   •   •

D

As he drums his heels on the floor of the aisle
between the peanut butters and the shelf
of cereals, this toddler's tantrums thrill
families of shoppers; his mother; even himself.

From time to time he pauses to overhear
the primitive howls he unleashes within the cage
of his wants. DESIRE is two years old in the head
hardwired at whatever age
to the gemlike flame of its needs
and shamelessly mewing it claws, kicks, kills
until it succeeds.

The carnival shuts down.
The farms go derelict.
The city sinks in gloom
from swinish neglect.

Playing the blues so blue
her anguish is exquisite
DESPAIR sits in the room
that passion never visits.

•   •   •

B

You thought it might be an Odalisque
oiling her body for the artist
or a slim strong boy still in his hairless phase
or a glimpse of pebbles
painstakingly raked to suggest the ocean.
Possibly the real ocean tranquil at sunset.

Instead

it is this great lumbering sow of a grizzly
two cubs hanging off her teats
this sow wearing a halo of insistent gnats
this great bear enslaved by her offspring
whom she must feed, shelter, teach
what to fear, where to defecate, how to hunt.

Say the word only once
and prepare to die for the truth:
BEAUTY in her coarse fur
alive with ticks, her snub snout
hooked claws, and so white teeth.

IV

·

·

·

NEW YEAR'S EVE 1959

remembering Anne Sexton and Jack Geiger

This was the way we used to party:
lamps unplugged, shoved in the closet
rugs rolled up, furniture pushed back
Glenn Miller singles on the spindle.

There was the poet kicking off her shoes
to jitterbug with the Physician
for Social Responsibility
the only time they ever met

and he pecking his head to the beat
swinging her out on the stalk of his arm
setting all eight gores of her skirt
twirling, then hauling her in for a Fred

Astaire session of deep dips
and both of them cutting out to strut
humming along with the riffs
that punctuated "Chattanooga Choo Choo."

This was after Seoul and before Saigon.
Coke was still a carbonated drink
we added rum to. There was French wine
but someone had misplaced the curlicue

and a not-yet famous novelist
magicked the cork out on the hinge
of the back door to "Sunrise Serenade"
and dance was the dark enabler.

Lights off a long minute at midnight
(squeals and false moans) madcap Anne
long dead now and Jack snowily
balding who led the drive to halt the bomb

and I alone am saved to tell you
how they could jive.

OCTOBER, YELLOWSTONE PARK

How happy the animals seem just now,
all reading the sweetgrass text, heads down
in the great yellow-green sea of the high plains—
antelope, bison, the bull elk and his cows

moving commingled in little clumps, the bull
elk bugling from time to time his rusty screech
but not yet in rut, the females not yet in heat,
peacefully inattentive—the late fall

asters still blooming, the glacial creeks running clear.
What awaits them this winter—which calves will starve
to death or driven by hunger stray from the park
to be shot on the cattle range—they are unaware.

It is said that dumb beasts cannot anticipate
though for terror of fire or wolves some deep
historical memory clangs out of sleep
pricking them to take flight. As flight pricked the poet

dead seventeen years today, who for seventeen
years before that was a better sister
than any I, who had none, could have conjured.
Dead by her own hand, who so doggedly whined

at Daddy Death's elbow that the old Squatter
at last relented and took her in. Of sane mind
and body aged but whole I stand by the sign
that says we are halfway between the equator

and the North Pole. Sad but celebratory
I stand in full sun on the 45th parallel
bemused by what's to come, by what befell,
by how our friendship flared into history.

Fair warning, Annie, there will be no more
elegies, no more direct-address songs
conferring the tang of loss, its bitter flavor
as palpable as alum on the tongue.

Climbing up switchbacks all this afternoon,
sending loose shale clattering below,
grimly, gradually ascending to a view
of snowcaps and geysers, the balloon

of Old Faithful spewing, I hear your voice
beside me (you, who hated so to sweat!)
cheerfully cursing at eight thousand feet
the killers of the dream, the small-time advice-

laden editors and hangers-on. I've come
this whole hard way alone to an upthrust slate
above a brace of eagles launched in flight
only to teeter, my equilibrium

undone by memory. I want to fling
your cigarette- and whiskey-hoarse chuckle
that hangs on inside me down the back wall
over Biscuit Basin. I want the painting

below to take me in. My world that threatened
to stop the day you stopped, faltered
and then resumed, unutterably altered.
Where wildfires crisped its hide and blackened

whole vistas, new life inched in. My map
blooms with low growth, sturdier than before.
Thus I abstain. I will not sing, except
of the elk and his harem who lie down in grandeur

on the church lawn at Mammoth Hot Springs,
his hat rack wreathed in mist. This year's offspring
graze in the town's backyards, to the dismay
of tenants who burst out to broom them away.

May the car doors of tourists slam, may cameras go wild
staying the scene, may the occasional
antelope slip into the herd, shy as a child.
May people be ravished by this processional.

May reverence for what lopes off to the hills
at dusk be imprinted on their brain pans
forever, as on mine. As you are, Anne.
All of you hammered golden against the anvil.

IN MEMORY OF DANNY L.

Magnetized
on the refrigerator
prideful in his new glasses

he smiles forth still
sounding out the first
parts of words then guessing

the rest and when his
third grade class laughed
at *cowbarn* for *coward*

he was pleased to laugh
with them who go forward
this year to junior high

so that after his heart
gave out that day
on the playground slide

carrying off the only
Downs child in his
village school this

same passport-size
photo went up in
a dozen houses to say

that he who had hugged
every dog, pony, lamb
had come and gone

and in some will adhere
as in ours
for years.

CARRYING SUE

in memory of Sue Dexter

Two women of a certain age, we met
at a clinic, not for weight loss
or substance abuse, but to learn
how to be better drivers of
the horses our bodies no longer
could comfortably bestride.

Rescuers, each of us knew
the awful passivity of
the starved or abandoned horse.
Awarded safe pasture, feed, shelter
he does not at first believe
his life has rebegun.

Weeks pass. Aloof and dumb
he suffers the hand's caress,
the farrier's tools, but slowly comes
back to us along lost pathways
that allow us to touch across
our separate species.

Her bitter gall so terrible
no one could touch her anguish
my friend lies dead
of a galloping leukemia.
She who raced me uphill
or overtook me on the flat,
our horses both hellbent for joy,
now lies uncomforted.

I have her driving apron
slick waterproof green on one side
riotous plaid on the other.
I still have her pair of spare reins
that easily thread through my terrets.

Each time I hitch up and vault into the cart
I call her back across lost pathways.
I carry her forth.

LANCASTER COUNTY

for Robin Becker

The sidewise cant of their ears
their bedslat skinny flanks
their flaccid tails laid flat
tell you these are Standardbreds

bought off the track and tied
to stand all market day
in a nagging refrain of flies
while rosy Amish women

brooding their stair-step children
lean over planked tables
to hawk homemade blood sausages
in their captive succulence.

You are the tourist in upstate PA
who buys a peck of windfall apples
and tempts, palm flat, the bitted creatures
who have never been hand-fed before

who wait to trot nine miles home
over the stinging asphalt
living acceptable engines that draw
the pillowed Amish in their bonnets

and buttoned-over pregnancies
inside the square black box on wheels.

AFTER THE POETRY READING

for Marie Howe

If Emily Dickinson lived in the 1990s
and let herself have sex appeal
she'd grow her hair wild and electric
down to her buttocks, you said. She'd wear
magenta tights, black ankle socks
and tiny pointed paddock boots.

Intrigued, I saw how Emily'd
master Microsoft, how she'd
fax the versicles that Higginson
advised her not to print to MS.
APR and Thirteenth Moon.

She'd read aloud at benefits
address the weavers' guild
the garden club, the anarchists
Catholics for free choice
welfare moms, the Wouldbegoods
and the Temple Sinai sisterhood.

Thinking the same thing, silent
we see Emily flamboyant.
Her words for the century to come
are pithy, oxymoronic.
Her fly buzzes me all the way home.

GUS SPEAKS

I was the last of my line,
farm-raised, chesty, and bold.
Not one of your flawless show-world
forty-five-pound Dalmatians.
I ran with the horses, my darlings.

I loped at their heels, mile
for mile, swam rivers they forded
wet to the belly. I guarded
them grazing, haloed in flies.
Their smell became my smell.

Joyous I ate their manure.
Its undigested oats
still sweet, kept me fit.
I slept curled at the flank
of the fiercest broodmare.

We lay, a study in snores
ear flicks and farts in her stall
until she came to the brink,
the birth hour of her foal.
Then, she shunned me cruelly.

Spring and fall I erred over
and over. Skunks were my folly.
Then, I was nobody's lover.
I rolled in dung and sand.
When my heart burst in the pond,

my body sank and then rose
like a birch log, a blaze
of white against spring green.

Now I lie under the grasses
they crop, my own swift horses

who start up and spook in the rain
without me, the warm summer rain.

FROM THE 18TH FLOOR

for Hilma Wolitzer

Sunrise is a peach curtain,
the river a woman
in a lamé dress. Noon, its
slats up, a wide heaven,
dusk a soundless
opera, orange-tinged.

Down there, people reduce
to insects, the dry pods
of their commonplace
griefs, desires, occasional
joys tiny ramrods
within the scuttle that propels
them so grace-
fully backwards and forwards.

We who are merely
the guests of insects,
twelve times outweighed
by them on this planet,
breathe lightly at the window.
We admire the clean
confusion below
such as God might have seen
circling at this height,
deciding not to land

so that when
the knife-scream of rescue wagons
comes faintly through glass
it is less a sound than
a shape, a passing caress
up here where we impend
keeping an aesthetic distance,
large old friends.

SPRING TRAINING

for Victor

Some things never change: the velvet flock
of the turf, the baselines smoothed to suede,
the ancient smell of peanuts, the harsh smack
the ball makes burrowing into the catcher's mitt.

Here in the Grapefruit League's trellised shade
you catch Pie Traynor's lofting rightfield foul
all over again. You're ten in Fenway Park
and wait past suppertime for him to autograph it

then race for home all goosebumps in the dark
to roll the keepsake ball in paraffin,
soften your secondhand glove with neat's-foot oil
and wrap your Louisville Slugger with friction tape.

The Texas Leaguers, whatever league you're in
still tantalize, the way they waver and drop.
Carl Hubbell's magical screwball is still
give or take sixty years unhittable.

Sunset comes late but comes, inexorable.
What lingers is the slender hook of hope.

BEANS BEANS BEANS

for Yann

My grandson and I are doing up the beans
together to be blanched, then frozen.
We are singing *beans beans beans*
they make you feel so mean
on the farm on the farm.
Last week he shaved his head at soccer camp
—immediate regret—already it
is fuzzing over with biracial curls.

The green beans are Provider, bush. The yellow,
Kentucky Wonder, pole. The way I sort
is for convenience: size, not species.
They make a lovely mix, as do Yann's genes.
I like to think someday the world will be
one color, more or less. The word
is heterosis, hybrid vigor,
from the Greek for alteration.

Consider these beans, meanwhile, Provider
podding early, each plant a sturdy city,
roots like subways fanning out. The later
Wonders wrap creatively around
whatever's been set out for them:
poplar saplings, wire, twine,
winding, crosshatching, hanging on,
tying knots like boyish sailors
scrambling up the rigging toward the sun.

Take this crop in aggregate
shading from churned butter with flecks
of palest green to forest green, and take
this boy who helps to top and tail
a basketful with me, a creature leaping
between bush and pole.

THE RIDDLE OF NOAH

You want to change your name. You're looking
for "something more suitable," words we can only guess
you've come by from television or teachers. All
your first-grade friends have names like Justin Mark
Caroline Emma or newly enrolled Xuan Loc
and yours, you sadly report, is Noah . . . nothing.

Noah *Hodges*, your middle name isn't nothing
your mother, named Hodges, reproves, but you go on looking.
Next day you are somebody else: Adam Stinger! The clock
turns back to my brother, Edward Elias, whose quest
to be named for his father (living names are death marks
on a Jewish child) was fulfilled by a City Hall

clerk. Peter Jr. went gladly to school all
unblessed. The names that we go by are nothing
compared to the names we are called. *Christ killer*! they mocked
and stoned me with quinces in my bland-looking
suburb. Why didn't I tattle, resist? I guessed
I was guilty, the only kid on my manicured block

who didn't know how to genuflect as we lock-
stepped to chapel at noontime. I was in thrall,
the one Jewish girl in my class at Holy Ghost
convent school. Xuan Loc, which translates as something
magical and tender—Spring Bud, a way of looking
at innocence—is awarded the gold bookmark

for reading more chapter-books than Justin Mark
or Noah, who now has tears in his eyes. No lack
of feeling here, a jealous Yahweh is looking
over his shoulder hissing, Be best of all.
What can be done to ease him? Nothing
makes up for losing, though love is a welcome guest.

Spared being burned at the stake, being starved or gassed,
like Xuan Loc, Noah is fated to make his mark,
suffer for grace through good works, aspire to something.
Half-Jewish, half-Christian, he will own his name, will unlock
the riddle of who he is: only child, in equal
measure blessed and damned to be inward-looking,

always slightly aslant the mark, like Xuan Loc.
Always playing for keeps, for all or nothing
in quest of his rightful self while the world looks on.

CONNECTING THE DOTS

I think Daddy
just dropped dead
(our son at five)
I'll drive the car
and now they drive
us living, the large

children home
a week at Christmas
ten days in August
posing for
the family snapshot
flanked by dogs.

We're assayed kindly
to see if we're
still competent
to keep house, mind
the calendar
connect the dots.

Well, we're still stack-
ing wood for winter
turning compost
climbing ladders
and they still love us
who overtake us

who want what's best
for us, who sound
(deep reservoirs
of patience) the way
we did, or like
to think we did.